Minot Judson Savage

These Degenerate Days

Minot Judson Savage

These Degenerate Days

ISBN/EAN: 9783744652131

Printed in Europe, USA, Canada, Australia, Japan

Cover: Foto ©ninafisch / pixelio.de

More available books at **www.hansebooks.com**

THESE DEGENERATE DAYS

BY

MINOT J. SAVAGE

"Not ten strong men th' enormous weight could raise,—
Such men as live in these degenerate days "
                                    Pope's HOMER

BOSTON
GEO. H. ELLIS, 141 FRANKLIN STREET
1887

To J. R. Lowell.

Wit, Humorist, Poet, Critic, Diplomat:
  How many and what jewels deck the crown
  That marks the kingship of thy fair renown,—
The only kingship that a democrat
Like thee could covet! But, when one has sat
  Upon thy throne of thought, and, looking down,
  Has seen men cringing at a monarch's frown,
Beside real power, how poor must seem all that!

I have been one content to sit and hear
  Thy lark-song falling from the upper air
    To cheer the vale to humble tasks assigned.
And still thy old notes echo in my ear;
  And, as I listen, earth grows very fair,
    While I take heart and hope for all mankind!

"God is not dumb, that he should speak no more;
If thou hast wanderings in the wilderness
And find'st not Sinai, 'tis thy soul is poor;
There towers the mountain of the Voice no less,
Which whoso seeks shall find."

LOWELL'S *Bibliolatres.*

"These Degenerate Days."*

O LOWELL, once thy ringing words
Were keen and flashing, like the swords
With which Jehovah's hosts clove down
The fierce Philistine's haughty crown!

In days when Liberty lay low,
Despair of friend and scorn of foe;
When o'er her, in exultant mood,
Stood Ill in liveried guise of Good;
When Commerce, if it had a soul,
Had traded it for Judas' dole;
When Fashion, in her high estate,
Spelled out success and called it great;

* Written on reading Lowell's "Credidimus Jovem Regnare" in the *Atlantic* for February, 1887.

When preachers, like false watch-dogs, bayed
To fright the Truth they had betrayed,—
Then thou, young David, with thy sling
Didst to his knees the giant bring,
And, filling Israel's foes with dread,
Dismay through all his cohorts spread!

Or — change the figure — when increased
The revel of the godless feast
That, like Belshazzar's, set the seal
Of bondage on God's commonweal;
When in the nation's capital
Reigned Slavery's high carnival,
Where all the lords of wealth and might
Led captive outlawed Truth and Right,
And e'en the Temple cups brought in
To grace the triumph of their sin,—
Then thy handwriting on the wall

Did all their stoutest hearts appall;
Their trembling lips, with oath or prayer,
Betrayed the unseen spectre there;
While, in the lines thy finger drew,
The tyrant God's swift judgment knew!

Or — change the figure once again —
When, on the field of fighting men,
The two great armies met,— the free
Stood face to face with Slavery;
When both sides claimed their cause divine,
And looked to heaven for a sign,—
Thou didst flash out,— thy streaming hair
A threatening comet on the air,—
And, flaming far across the night,
Helped men believe God loved the right,
And, cleaving all the darkness through,
Wast herald of a day-dawn new!

How well do I recall the days
When, groping the uncertain ways
Then trodden by a country youth
Who tried to find and follow Truth,
While looking for some brain-refection
Within the meagre town collection
That all its scanty wealth made free
To hungry comers for a fee,
I stumbled on a rare surprise,—
A book so witty and so wise
That ever since I've venerated
The man who *Hosea B.* created,
And taught him how, with speech uncouth,
To make me hate aught less than truth,
And with his ringing challenge lead
The way to noble thought and deed!
He bade me hate the coward lie,
That good with yesterday could die;

He bade revere the noble past,
Yet know no partial form could last;
He bade me know that each fresh morn
Some new God-gotten truth is born,
And but the future shall unfold
Man's blessed hope, the age of gold!
His words, that shamed all halting fear,
How oft they've rung in my glad ear!—
New visions that God gives to youth
Still make the "ancient good uncouth";
And they must "onward, upward still,"
Who hope Truth's mission to fulfil;
We like the Pilgrims still must be,
And "launch our 'Mayflower' on the sea,"
Nor think "the Past's blood-rusted key"
Can ope the doors of destiny!

Alas! whose is this weary wail
That but repeats the outworn tale

That, in each age since time began,
Has mocked the growing hope of man?
As far back as old Homer's days,
They had begun this plaint to raise,
And, sighing on through senile rhymes,
To maunder of "degenerate" times.
The poet old, as up the track
Of years heroic he looked back,
Beheld the figures looming tall
About the Trojans' fated wall,
And sad exclaimed, "Not ten strong men —
Alas! the world is not as then —
Could now e'en lift the rock that he,
Great Ajax, tossed so easily!"
And ever since, the ages long,
Has echoed down the same old song.
Each age repeats its wonder-lore
Of wonder people gone before;

Sees, looming huge the twilight through,
Shapes that no present ever knew.
If one believed the tales, he'd think
The world was ever on the brink
Of some *Ragnarok*, doomed to be
The dwindled earth's catastrophe!
And yet, somehow, in logic's spite,
The earth rolls upward through the night,
And every day, with promise new,
The sun shines out, and heaven is blue!

E'en in my life,— not long as yet,—
So many times the day's been set
When this old world, so doomed to evil,
So hastening downward to the devil,
Was just about its grip on bliss
To lose, and plunge adown th' abyss;
And yet, so often, when I've placed

Myself, and got my feet well braced,
In waiting for the world's undoin',
They have postponed the final ruin,
That I've concluded now to wait
Until does strike the clock of fate,
And not waste time, with fret and fume,
Until I hear the "crack o' doom"!
For, though these dismal prophets tell
Each time will be the "last" farewell,
The ruined earth comes smiling up
To pledge us in a brimming cup
Of God's new wine of life, that runs
Cheer-giving rays of brighter suns!

O Lowell! no one better knows
That slavery of the body grows
From slavery of heart and mind,—
That both are ever of a kind!

And yet the blast that thou couldst blow,
That so rocked Slavery's Jericho,—
Alas! one scarce believes his ears,—
Now pipes, an echo of the fears
Of these same Canaanites, who quake
When Israel's rams' horns music make!

For this same Science that has pried,
That questions earth and heaven beside,
That, like the Babel-builders, frets
God's fearful champions with its threats
Of scaling heaven, and flinging down
The weak Almighty's rusty crown,—
Alas! the poor Omnipotence
That seems to need such hot defence!—
This Science is the Titan strong,
Prometheus, who, to right man's wrong,
To lift the weak, and haste the hour

When thought should triumph over power,
Defied the hate conservative,
That he to daring souls might give
The fire celestial, raising clods
Till they should come to be like gods!
Since man, of every force the slave,
Crept, an autochthon, from his cave,
And, brutal, fought with brute, to share
His uncooked food and bedless lair,
Until, a Jesus, God's own child,
He walked the old earth undefiled,—
Until, with Shakspere's fancy, he
His home made in eternity,—
Until the measured suns confess
Him child of the Almightiness,—
Until the steam, winds, lightnings, all
Of nature's forces, know his call,—
Until, in spite of craven fears,

He's climbed the summit of the years,
And, fearless of the "pious" frown,
Has seized and worn his manhood's crown,—
From that far time till this, pray tell
What problem he has tried to spell
But some voice still has filled his ears
With boding wail and threatening fears?
And yet each step that nearer brought
The goal of good was science-taught.
It meant the wider, freer mind,
That to near dangers could be blind,
And dare to see a better day
Break with its promise far away!
But never a new morning broke
Except to hear the troubled croak
Of some belated bird of night,
That thought day ended with the light!

See man, a brute half-waked from sleep,
Along his shores primeval creep,
And, awe-struck, scan the misty deep!
And now, behold! the dug-out boat,
In which he dared the waves to float,
To palaces steam-driven grown!
Lo! man has made the sea his throne,
While storms and winds his vassals are,
Which, harnessed to his floating car,
Bring all earth's treasures from afar!

See man, fear-cowed, his hands upraise
To where the clouds with lightnings blaze,
While his distorted fancy sees
A dragon red devour the trees;
And he, with prayers and gifts, in vain
The monster's ravage would restrain!
And now, behold! the lightnings run,

From rising until set of sun
On tireless feet, his willing slave,
Climb mountains, dive beneath the wave,
Till, distancing the weary wind,
E'en Puck's fleet wings are left behind!

See man, unclothed, a tree-branch tear
To fight the nature-weaponed bear,
And rob him of his blood-stained skin
To wrap his freezing weakness in!
And now, behold! the walls arise
Of countless humming factories,
Where willing waterfalls their play
To restless labor turn all day;
Or where the steam, as in delight,
Puts forth its never-wearied might,
With ponderous stroke, or gentle tap
Too low to rouse a sick man's nap!

And see, almost surpassing thought,
The crude to shapes of beauty wrought.
How like a god of power profuse
It pours its gifts for human use!

See man, whose babblings vainly reach
To grasp the mystery of speech,
With cry and gesture seeking still
Some fuller utterance of his will,
While, like a muddy pool, his brain,
Distorted, gives no image plain!
And now, behold! the alphabet
Like gems upon his brow he's set,
And his expanding brain he's taught
To form and echo subtlest thought.
Next, from the mine, that wondrous thing,
A pen he's borrowed for a wing.
With this through fancy's realm he flies

Or soars in philosophic skies;
With Dante sweeps the dusky air
That's heavy with a soul's despair;
Or, with the blind old seer for guide,
Looks down o'er heaven's champaign wide;
With Kepler, where God's planets are,
Tracks God's own thought from star to star,
Or dives down to the depths to see
The microscope's infinity.
As thus by growing thought portrayed,
Man seems but less than angel made!

See man to fetich bending low,
And seeing in each force a foe.
The gods his enemies appear;
His worship's but a cringing fear:
In blood, in sorrow, tears, and hate,
He solves the riddle of his fate.

Upon a bleeding altar piled,
He burns his slave, his wife, his child,—
The dearest and the best,—to buy
The cruel gods that sit on high.
And now, behold! the shapes of hate
That brooded o'er his hapless fate
Have faded from the heavens bright,
As day drives off the scowling night.
And all these many, grown to one,
Shine on us like a risen sun.
Now hear we the apostle's call,
"One God and Father of us all";
And, knowing we're one brotherhood,
Learn that God's worship means man's good,
While, looking up the years, we see
God's and man's kingdom that's to be!

It asks no learning recondite
To trace the dawn of all this light.

'Tis Science, free thought, just the grace
That dared to look God in the face,
That dared to question heaven and earth,
That brings the God-man child to birth.
'Tis this that stole the heavenly spark,
And made man victor o'er the dark;
'Tis this that over earth and sea
Has given him the victory;
'Tis this, with power to loose and bind,
That's made him king of steam and wind;
'Tis this that cleared the forests dread,
And gave the farm and park instead;
'Tis this that forged the lightning's chain,
And with it girdled land and main;
'Tis this that, linking thought to speech,
Brings earth and heaven within his reach;
'Tis this that humanizes God,
And shows of kin with him the clod!

The whole long reach from brute to man
That binds the ages with its span,
That reaches forward till we see
The better time that is to be,—
All this long tale of battles won
But tells what God-led thought has done!
And not one single step was taken
But some old structure still was shaken.
And its self-styled defender's gloom
Mistook Truth's tread for "trump of doom."

But, Lowell, had it been foretold
That you'd have played this farce so old,
Though prophets had declared they knew it,
I'd never have believed you'd do it!
For all these years thy trumpet-blast
Has led me onward from the past,
While ever o'er the conflict's gloom

Far in the van I've seen thy plume;
And, while thy bugle note still rung,
In brain and heart I've known thee young.
I would have sworn, whoever faltered,
My Lowell's faith and trust unaltered.
So, when I saw thee in the rear,
I cried, "What god has struck with fear
My hero?" And with heart all pain
I felt "my eyes cloud up for rain."

When Douglass, on the trial day,
Felt once his faith and trust give way,
Up rose brave old Sojourner Truth,
With face of coal and form uncouth,
But with a soul devoid of fear,
And rang out with her challenge clear:
"Shame, Frederick, in your panic dread!
Say, dost thou think that God is dead?"

Alas, poor God! whose servants fear
That, like a cloud, he'll disappear,
If some new thought should dare to frame
For his old power some newer name!
Alas, poor God! that such transition
Should hinge upon a definition!
Art thou so weak some fatal spasm
May seize thee, if called protoplasm?
And did brave Cromwell's power, that sent
Fear-stricken a whole parliament,
That, spite of awe that hedged a king,
Could Charles unto a scaffold bring,—
Was all this power on him conferred
By just the difference in a word?

'Tis very, very sweet indeed,
This peace and quiet of one's creed;
To hear "Old Hundred" ringing loud,

As if from angels on a cloud;
To feel the soul, on lifted wing,
Soar upward as the people sing,—
These sentiments are passing dear,
As were those strains to childhood's ear.
But who'd not gladly give this peace,
If so the world might gain release
From that old horror of the hell
That all the ancient creeds foretell?
"Old Hundred," even, had the moan
Of lost souls for an undertone:
One still heard, in its grandest strains,
The drip of tears and clank of chains.
From the old record can we strike
Just what we happen not to like,—
Keep the old mansion, but let go
The shadowy basement down below?

Your brother poet, Holmes, whose head
With all our loves is garlanded,—
He, too, not long since, spoke his mind
About our modern Thomas-kind.
He called them "mystery-solving lynxes,"
And sighed for old times, when the sphinxes
Looked calmly o'er the dreaming sand
Of Egypt's still undoubting land.
He cried, "Give back our faith!" The ways
They used to know in convent days
Were better than this finding out
The truth, whose shadow still is doubt!

True, true, if turning on our track
The ancient comfort might bring back;
If — this is Tennyson's heart-cry,
When dawn was fading from his sky —
If we "our sister's heaven" might know

Without our brother's hell of woe;
If we might tread the old-time path,
And find the love without the wrath,—
Oh, then it might be sweet indeed
To "robe us" in our outworn creed!
But is't not something, when all's done,
The cursing of the curse t' have won?
If th' agnostic gives not bliss,
Yet who will not be glad at this,—
That one may dare to doubt th' abyss?

If there lives one who breathes man's breath
Who would not welcome dreamless death,
Who would not kiss the grave's green sod
And glad embrace the senseless clod,
Who'd not with gratitude lay down
His hope of heaven and his crown,
And, like a miser, grasp and keep

The poor blank hope of endless sleep,—
This, rather than take heaven's fee
At cost of hopeless misery
Of one poor soul, the meanest one
That ever crawled beneath the sun,—
If there is one such selfish soul
Who o'er one lost would reach his goal,
Then I in hell would rather be
Than share e'en heaven with such as he!

Let me then live my poor life out
Befogged and lost on seas of doubt
Rather than by hell's light to see
A "title clear" to bliss for me!
And He who, as the churches say,
To save men left the realms of day,
Sure He'll not love me less for this,
That I'd surrender all my bliss

To go among the lost and take
A cooling drop their thirst to slake!
Or can it be that now so long
He's listened to the gladsome song
Of those far off from pain, his ears
Grow deaf to sounds of falling tears?

But are we quite lost in the fog?
Do never angels go *incog.*?
Sometimes — the Bible so declares —
Men "entertain them unawares."
Perhaps this Science men so fear
God's guiding angel may appear.
In every step the world has taken,
The ancient things are always shaken;
And what is shaken, Scriptures say,
Is just about to pass away.
The old must change and pass, 'tis true,

But only to make room for new.
The plough must May's fresh flowers tear
That it the harvest may prepare;
And, if a mouse's nest be torn,
The end of all the mouse may mourn:
And yet the harvest justifies
The deaths that in its pathway lies.
'Twas undue love for older thought
That Jesus to Golgotha brought;
For he the rough disturber seemed
Of sweet old rest in which men dreamed.
And they who now the new deride
Still shout, "Let him be crucified!"
The ages change; but still men slay
The daring prophets of their day,
While ancient slayers they disdain,
And laud the victims once so slain.
Alas, such "difference should be

'Twixt tweedledum and tweedledee"!
But Tweedledum is old; and so
About it ancient ivies grow.
While Tweedledee is new: as yet
The ivy leaves are hardly set.

"O ye of little faith!" d'ye fear
God cannot face the daylight clear,
That he's a God of cloud and night,
And dreads the dawn's uprising light?
Art fearful that his work may show
Brass 'neath the gilt to those who know,—
That to a strict search there might be
Found aught to shame the deity?
Is this world but an empty shrine
That hides within it naught divine?
Must they who'd their devotion keep
From far, through half-shut eyelids, peep

At his high temple, guarded well
By priests who know, but dare not tell,
Lest, should they tell, all men would know
That they are orphans here below?
Oh, sure, this doubt of truth must be
The one, real infidelity!
God must possess omnipotence,
Or he'd be slain by such defence!
And, Father, in thy book write down —
I never tried to save thy crown,
But trusted that thy throne was sure,
Rock-based in that which must endure!

At sea we sail; nor yet may know
The port,— whence come nor where we go.
Sometimes the sun laughs on our way;
Sometimes we're glad to lose the day,
Because the wide night-heaven, afire

With stars, may teach us to aspire.
Sometimes the fog devours the sun,
And e'en the stars fade, one by one.
But what man ever cast a log
Who does not know *light makes the fog ?*
Light is above, below, around ;
And, though the dismal fog-bell sound,
Still hold the helm, and forward glide,
Steam onward towards the farther side.
For there the sun smiles, and in glee
The winds play with the laughing sea.
'Tis but the coward who turns back,
And shirks the God-appointed track.
Through cloud or sun drive on the keel ;
'Tis God, though unseen, holds the wheel.
Or, if one doubts this, playing trust
Will naught avail us: sink we must.

I fret not, though, with flattened nose
Against the pane, "beyond my toes"
I cannot see : the track behind
Such ages long, through wave and wind,
Some hand has guided, that I know
The helmsman cannot be my foe.
The seas we have sailed over tell
The hand that holds us knows them well.
Still brighter stars shine out at night;
Still fairer countries heave in sight;
And, by the warrant of the past,
Some noble port we'll make at last!

Or, let us sink, the power that wakes
The wind song, or with morning breaks,
Still whispers to the ear that hears
More than to hasty sight appears,—
Assurance that, though wrecked, 'twould be
To sail still on —"another sea."

O Lowell! I gave first to thee
My boyhood's love and loyalty.
My youth took fire at thy word;
And thou my manhood's spirit stirred
To lofty faith and noble trust.
I love thee still, because I must;
For early loves and trusts remain,
Nor break with common stress or strain.
Among the singers who have made
Rare music in each wood and glade
Of our New England, thy heart tone
Has oftenest matched and thrilled my own.
Wherever storming party led,
I've seen thy standard still ahead;
Wherever fight was fought for man,
I've heard thy shout far in the van.
And now — I cannot bear to think
The hour should come when thou wouldst
    shrink,

Cry halt, or lose that courage grand
That gave thy voice its old command.

And dost thou fear that, science-led,
The world may find that Faith is dead,—
Exchange the soul for dust, and see
No more the stars that used to be?
No, no! Thou canst not! For to-day
The old-time "faiths" do pass away;
But Faith remains; and, undefiled,
True Science is true Faith's own child.
She only dares, with utter trust,
To seek God in a grain of dust,
And learn that sainthood's holiest awe
Is one with gravitation's law.
She only dares, and, daring, holds
That *One Life* all the worlds enfolds;
And that, or studying soul or clod,

We still are face to face with God;
That, spell it ever as we will,
It is the same One Being still;
That, in the soul or in a sun,
The one same force is ever one;
That, though all else be less than sure,
This basis is at least secure.

And dost thou really fear to see
In science death of poetry?
I know that Wordsworth, in his age,
Was senile grown instead of sage,
And, careless of God's new worlds born,
Bemoaned lost "Triton" and his "horn,"
So fearful was he lest the Muse
To flee a wiser world should choose.
But is this Poesy a sprite
To flee, ghost-like, the morning's light?

Must she still prattle on in rhymes
That sing of only child-world times?
Or is she not God's daughter grave,
With star-like eyes, and girded brave
With God's breastplate of truth, to sing
The grander ages and their king?
The baby-house that man once taught
Was measure of th' Almighty thought,
The petty world that Dante knew,
Our daring Science has burst through;
While up star-vistas now we see
The gateways of Infinity.
Shall not the Muse some day be heard
In utterance of a grander word,
To match the grander theme that runs,
A fugue, whose notes are worlds and suns?

Could she but tune her mighty lyre,
And prelude first the cloud of fire

That, cooling, one by one has whirled
Off ring on ring, each ring a world;
Could she sing thus the planet's birth,
And how life dawned upon the earth;
Could she the mystery unfold
Of how the new succeeds the old;
See man leap to his feet, and face
The heavens, and then his journey trace,
As on, through blood and toil and tears,
He climbed the steep path of the years,
Until, with earth beneath his feet,
He stood divine, a man complete,—
Could but the Muse, instead of whining
For what returns not for repining,
But plume her wing for this high flight,
She might a poem still indite,
Compared with which the epics old,
That chant a dreamed-of "age of gold,"

Were but as dawn-time twitterings
Matched with the song the skylark sings.

So, Lowell, strike thy harp once more,
And let us hear it as of yore —
Such music as once cheered the slave,
Made cowards hide or else turn brave.
The sun is not about to set;
'Tis but the morning twilight yet.
The dawn still fights the early mists:
But 'tis Apollo in the lists;
And his bright arrows shall lay low
The Dragon, Dark, his ancient foe.
Man's but a child as yet; but see
The cradled Hercules to be,
Who e'en with infant hands can slay
The serpent ills that cross his way.

Behind us is the dawn ; before,
The day is broadening to more;
And man, the child of all the past,
Approaches man's estate at last.
"Now are we sons of God!" nor see
But glimpses of the yet to be,—
The glory that shall come to birth
When man's at one with God on earth.
Then, Lowell, let thy latest lay
Be not a wail of dying day;
But let us hear thy bugle-horn
Ring welcome to the rising morn.